821.91 O'DRI   03/09   © 16.3
3*

KU-524-791

Hidden Extras

WITHDRAWN
FROM
MIC-SPCT

St Patrick's College
Thurles
01623

03/09.

16.3
53✳

Dennis O'Driscoll

Hidden Extras

Anvil Press Poetry

Published in 1987
by Anvil Press Poetry Ltd
69 King George Street London SE10 8PX
and 27 South Main Street Wolfeboro NH 03894 USA
in a co-edition with Dedalus Press, Dublin

Copyright © Dennis O'Driscoll 1987

This book is published
with financial assistance from
The Arts Council of Great Britain

Set in Joanna
by Bryan Williamson, Manchester
Printed in Great Britain
at The Arc & Throstle Press, Todmorden, Lancs

British Library Cataloguing in Publication Data

O'Driscoll, Dennis
  Hidden extras.
  I. Title
  821'.914   PR6065.D/

Library of Congress Cataloging-in-Publication Data

O'Driscoll, Dennis.
  Hidden extras.

  I. Title.
PR6065.D75H5 1987   821'.914   87-1046

ISBN 0-85646-190-3

Coláiste
Mhuire Gan Smál
Luimneach

Class	821.91
Suff	ODR
MI	

FOR JULIE

ACKNOWLEDGEMENTS

Acknowledgements are due to the Arts
Council/An Chomhairle Ealaíon for a helpful
bursary and, for first publishing some of these
poems, to *Agenda*, *Buff* (New York), *The Echo-Room*,
Edinburgh Review, *The Irish Times*, *London Magazine*, *New
Statesman*, *Oxford Poetry*, *Paris/Atlantic*, *Poetry Australia*,
Poetry Ireland Review, *Poetry Review* and *Times Literary
Supplement*.
 'Time Sharing' and 'Normally Speaking' were
first published in *Poetry* (Chicago).
 Part Two contains versions of seven poems
from *Kist* (Dolmen Press, 1982).

CONTENTS

PART TWO

Part One

FIRST IMPRESSIONS

Open the hall door
and let the year's first sunlight in,
picking its way through coal seams of darkness:
a gleaming copper hot-water pipe;
a bale of wheaten straw;
a hose of light drenching our chambered mound.

Hard green supermarket pears mellow on the window-sill.
One blackbird still gives preference to our cul-de-sac.
Bedroom-pink cherry and hawthorn talc are visible
after steam baths of fog and rain,
only a powdery, eye-shadow cloud
now smudged under sun.

Bad pennies, earth's small change,
the dandelions are scattered everywhere.
Oval buds begin to hatch.
And the sun slips in through the front door,
restoring our storm-battered house,
converting it into a holiday home.

G-PLAN ANGST

He has everything.
A beautiful young wife.
A comfortable home.
A secure job.
A velvet three-piece suite.
A metallic-silver car.
A mahogany cocktail cabinet.
A rugby trophy.
A remote-controlled music centre.
A set of golf clubs under the hallstand.
A fair-haired daughter learning to walk.

What he is afraid of most
and what keeps him tossing some nights
on the electric underblanket,
listening to the antique clock
clicking as if with disapproval from the landing,
are the stories that begin:
He had everything.
A beautiful young wife.
A comfortable home.
A secure job.
Then one day.

HERE AND NOW

There's a mirror that has seen me
for the last time—BORGES

There are poems I could write only in the present tense
that I will never be in a position to again:
about looking into a mirror and seeing not one grey hair
or sitting with you in an unburgled living room,
the terminal diseases still dormant in our cells.

Or there is the poem of this very moment,
sunset streaking the horizon like a circus poster,
the sky wearing a v-neck of homing geese,
bubbles of fleece blowing from dandelion and thistle,
a wasp in jockey colours racing the dark.

There is the poem of this unrecorded second,
so nondescript, so tame, so plain:
the smack of a gardener's spade, a distracting hum,
radio jingles leaching through a parked car;
and now a milkman's helper is distributing bills.

Somewhere else, locked in our past tense, beyond grasp,
first lovers thrill to mutual discoveries
—beginnings we too recall, pristine invigorating dawns
fresh as if earth's architect just left,
cloud's mortar setting above building-rubble hills.

And elsewhere, too, a world of frenzy: commodity markets,
blackberry riot police, crises of age and youth.
The unwrinkled glass that holds me in the balance
between past and future is a river I must cross,
floating out of depth towards its unreflective side.

DUMB CREATURES

autistic turtles are rent from their husks
the Himalayan musk's anus is raided for cosmetics
boiling pots of jellyfish spill over into oil

the rhino's horn is ground as aphrodisiac
tanned snakeskin tempts the Eden-seeking tourists
lizard wallets clasp their cash, elephant legs make trash cans

oryx and leopard blaze out of guns' telescopic sights
wildflowers draw their petal blinds tight
toadspawn drained from ponds, corncrakes harvested

and butchered human skulls heap up like coral souvenirs
or the tiers of sterile eggs left unhatched by sea birds
on the beaches of atomic-test atolls

READER'S DIGEST FAMILY MEDICAL ADVISER

'An A-Z Guide to Everyday Ailments'

Everyday asthma and brain tumour.
Everyday chilblains, cancers, coronaries.
Everyday depression and epilepsy.
Everyday falls and gallstones.
Everyday Hodgkin's Disease and insomnia.
Everyday jaundice, keratosis, leukaemia.
Everyday multiple sclerosis, nephritis, ovarian cyst.
Everyday polio, pneumonia, quinsy, rheumatic pain.
Everyday syphilis, threadworm, ulcer, varicose vein.

Six hundred and twenty-four pages long.
Three columns wide.
One size fits all.

TWO SILENCES

I

his morning calls over, my father drives outside the town
he parks beside a rusty gate tied with baling twine
I can see shy daisies eyeing me from a lush coat of green
we unpack lunch with the car windows down
the sandwiches my mother made taste creamy and fresh
we dine in perfect silence
I smell the dark vapour from his coffee flask
and drink tickling lemonade from a chipped cup
there are slices of chocolate swiss-roll for dessert
and a banana ripening into cheetah spots
a breeze brings goosebumps to the barks
of trees that toss their heads of leaves back
to form chintzy lampshades for the sun
we take our ease, breadcrumbs hardening in our laps

II

my father was turning away from life exiled in pain
harder to locate with each hospital visit
drumming sonatas of impatience on a bedside locker
shuffling among dressing-gowned wraiths
whose slippers had worn the corridor linoleum to a blur:
once after he was given day-clothes back
I searched the gloomy wood-panelled billiards room
and the tacky shop of evening papers and Good Luck cards
a summer shower was drooping at the time I found him
on a remote bench beneath a patulous tree
ground staff clattered past with rake and barrow
in the recreation hall the chaplain would be tuning the TV
out at sea the mail boat was dissolving into mist
as I came near he turned the other way

RESIDUARY ESTATES

I

an unprimed canvas perhaps
with its first dab of paint
or abstract expressionism
this tainted stool
streaked with blood
a red stripe
worthy of Barnett Newman

an ideogram for death

II

cancerous cells are immortal
laboratory tests suggest

is this the everlasting life
my mother now enjoys

that she had prayed for:
the life beyond the grave

DISTURBING MY MOTHER

It has been ten years since our last direct exchange
and I have not dared to interrupt your rest.
It is so long since we were one family,
talking together in one inviolable room.

Our silence now is like a Sunday afternoon at home
with you taking your weekly break, dozing by the fire,
the newspaper sliding down your knees,
your face palsied by twitching flames.

A decade ago your grating final breath
like a rasping gate admitted death
and we set off on our own, your offspring,
a hunted, howling, endangered flock.

On the anniversary of your assimilation into pain,
I am referred to the same hospital for an x-ray
and find another family weeping inside the door
appalled at the indifference sweeping past.

'You're finished', the radiographer announces
and instructs me to put back my clothes and leave.
My future prospects have shown up clearly:
a ghost, free of flesh, uniting you and me.

I await the medical results as I once waited
for exam reports during tense summer holidays,
going over the symptoms in my head, like maths,
to calculate whether I pass or fail.

Everything seems possible on this Sunday morning
as sun penetrates the silence, heats the garden seat,
and a bird pumped full of song
suppresses knowledge of life's hidden extras.

Your routine of cooking, cleaning, tending, caring
ended with skin's grain invaded by malignant knots,
wheeled in an enamel dish towards the mortuary slab,
a cold meat salad smothered in a lettuce of wreaths.

SIBLINGS REVISITED

I   DECLAN AT TWENTY

Only a few years ago, it was Jennings schoolboy stories
that I brought you. Now, I pack avant-garde books:
Tom Mallin, Alan Burns, a B.S. Johnson play.

'There isn't enough enthusiasm in the world', you always
      tell me.
And yours is revealed, petitioning for the release of prisoners,
contributing a series entitled 'Freedom' to The Tipperary Star,
reading African novelists, surveying a heron's nest,
displaying your unframed paintings along the bedroom wall.
In one corner, where a cliff of rock magazines used to rise,
back issues of New Statesman pile—the town's sole subscriber.
Of late, you have taken to playing the trumpet,
scorning sheet music in favour of the improvised tune.

You were maturing, swelling with cells, as parental death
      loomed,
called twice from the classroom for grim news.
I hint at the advantages of further studies sometimes.
Without success. And out of your seasonal job, of bog work,
you pay for essentials: subscriptions, membership fees, jazz LPs.
On blustery days, I wonder if the wind is with or against you
as you cycle there, along unsheltered miles....

Play me, improvise on the trumpet, the rhythm of your new life.
Blast me the notes of your freedom.
Show me how to extend past experience to joy.

II   EITHNE AT EIGHTEEN

The local paper carries your photograph this week,
at work collating parish registers of baptisms and marriages.
But death is the category you first kept records of.

I remember you waiting in the spacious hc
too young to visit our mother's cancer war
though old enough to know the worst.
Then growing up to watch our father's gra[
decline so rapidly towards the grave;
to buy school clothes with an executor's ch

Flush with saved earnings from your tempo
you can afford to join me in the city for a d
greeting me with a huge smile,
trying on endless styles in department store

You edge your way into the world with relish,
needing only a little support at this stage,
wanting only to channel your ardency
into one of the scores of jobs you patiently apply for
while vast untapped talent drains down the dole queues.

Enjoy the long evenings of these first post-school days.
Sleep well in our parents' ample bed.
That warm smile you surrender generously
has been achieved against the greatest odds.

SHELTER

for *Seamus*

The earth's tilted record spins and spins,
playing its warped old military tunes

while, at my brother's nursery, a pheasant nests,
its tail wing scarcely visible in shrubs.

Beneath is a stockpile of fourteen khaki eggs.
As spring's arsenal is kindled, throwing flames,

my brother is weeding plots out, training shoots,
digging trenches, inspecting drills.

Detonated shells litter the ground;
young pheasants manoeuvre through camouflage brush.

A squadron of goggled bees is buzzing the aubrietia;
I scan for threatening zeppelins of cloud.

WORDS FOR W.S. GRAHAM (1918-1986)

When I tap on the wall of your language,
who will be there to signal back?
What wordlouse will go scurrying between lines?

The twenty-six letters I conscript
cannot combine
to make themselves heard
above your silence.
My cursive waves break.
The water-table of language has run low.

You once wrote to say
how pleased you were
to have met me
at the Third Eye Centre in Glasgow
—where I have never been.
Address me now from where you are
—and where I have yet to see.
Speak with a sixth sense, a third eye.

Words are tonguetied by your defection.
Listen. Even the silence is silenced.
The language hides and seeks you.

NORMALLY SPEAKING

To assume everything has meaning.
To return at evening
feeling you have earned a rest
and put your feet up
before a glowing TV set and fire.
To have your favourite shows.
To be married to a local
whom your parents absolutely adore.
To be satisfied with what you have,
the neighbours, the current hemline,
the dual immersion, the government doing its best.
To keep to an average size
and buy clothes off the rack.
To bear the kind of face
that can be made-up to prettiness.
To head contentedly for work
knowing how bored you'd be at home.
To book holidays to where bodies blend,
tanned like sandgrains.
To be given to little excesses,
Christmas hangovers, spike high heels,
chocolate éclair binges, lightened hair.
To postpone children until the house extension
can be afforded and the car paid off.
To see the world through double glazing
and find nothing wrong.
To expect to go on living like this
and to look straight forward. No regrets.
To get up each day neither in wonder nor in fear,
meeting people on the bus you recognise
and who accept you, without question, for what you are.

WHAT SHE DOES NOT KNOW IS

That she is a widow.
That these are the last untinged memories of her life.
That he is slumped in his seat at a lay-by.
That a policeman is trying to revive him.
That the knife and fork she has set are merely decorative.
That the liver beside the pan will be left to rot.
That he has lost his appetite.
That the house she is tidying is for sale.
That the holiday photograph will be used for his memorial
   card.
That his sunburned body will not be subjected to direct
   light again.
That she will spend all night brewing tears.
That it is not his car she will soon hear slowing down outside.

Coláiste Mhuire Gan Smál Luimneach
81623

SERVING TIME

Fulfilling the forecast on the breakfast radio,
pods of hail were shelled on window ledges.
A wind that would whittle headstones
down to bones still rages as this poem
comes to you live from the second floor.
I take my place in the commentary box.

Here we all congregate at public hatch and desk:
the skinny spectacled clerk
with the Tupperware-packed lunch;
the new recruit, earnest in rolled-up sleeves;
the *True Romance* and thriller readers;
the lazy supervisor trying to command respect.

To work is to pray
but days stretch long and monotonous
as eternity, in my narrow cell,
with the pages of my office
perched on the wooden pew
or borne down long contemplative corridors.

I toil without hope of seeing God
or any parallel to God,
having groped from darkness summoned by bells
(the alarm clock's halo luminous)
and by the plainsong of birds
unbinding, note by note, the night.

Look around this claustral retreat:
you cannot miss the two steel presses,
one seething with memos, the other hoarding forms;
and a cabinet with deckled piles of correspondence
from banks, local authorities, accountancy firms.
I am undisputed Lord of the Files.

Straight opposite my varnished casket
is an A4 poster of Pasternak
(now weathered so that vernal green
has faded to autumnal beige)
and a plain Civil Service-issue calendar
listlessly heralding a new year.

I can be contacted here on weekdays
except during vacations and lunch.
Telephone queries, staff consultations
interrupt this script; and horns, hydraulic sneers,
sirens whimpering like hurt dogs
join in from South Great George's Street.

It is not much of a life,
serving time, applying directives or laws,
and therefore not much of a poem,
though revelation strikes occasionally:
a glimmer of wisdom shimmering on my coatstand,
an inkling of transcendence in a momentary hush.

Look through my desk with me:
stamps and staples, official envelopes, twine,
press cuttings, address books, unspent holiday coins.
What was it I set out to find?
A pair of brown shoelaces? The spare house key?
The secrets of the universe?

Look out across the two small apertures:
you can watch the backs of other blocks,
unsurpassed in wretchedness. One cube of glass
reflects sky, songless birds and slipping sun;
and I can make out clustered heads,
eggs incubating within the metal combs.

Will they ever metamorphose and float away?
Open the window a little before it steams. Look.
Gulls dipping for tea-break crusts
evoke unfrequented shores with skuas, kittiwakes;
wings trimming uneven hems of waves;
chestnut streams charging untamed.

Although I surge routinely on,
greeting familiar faces in the same place,
espying the same familiar strangers in the streets,
changes do occur, marked by collections, whip-rounds.
The amended staff-sheet instructs us to delete
the name of one girl, killed cycling from work.

As these last words are relayed to you,
my watch's nervous tic advances on half-five;
and I exit past the check-in clock where red blobs glow,
like tail lights in the traffic home
or votive lamps we lit as children
praying for a favourable exam result, a steady job.

OFFICE PHOTOGRAPH

for Margaret O'Sullivan

There will be no reunion for this class of people:
some are dead already; one immured in a convent;
others ill, retired, transferred, settled abroad.

But, for the duration of this photograph,
a fresh, foot-stamping morning reigns
(a few wear overcoats) and in the foreground

a wiry tree is barbed with buds.
Behind us, sun disperses shadows
of venetian blinds, like prison bars, on desks

and projects the film of dust specks
fidgeting on our stacked backlog of files.
We stare, smiling and clear-eyed, into a pensionable future.

Dressed in our best and at companionable ease,
we stand oblivious of how such scenes
will flash before us, recalling features

out of memory's frame, blurred by moving time;
and how this tableau, so tranquil in spring light,
so fixed in a known hour and place,

will develop into a focal point of change
as news comes of some name we match, then,
to a placid, frank, unwary face.

MAN GOING TO THE OFFICE

(a painting by Fernando Botero)

They all rush to the windows as he leaves.

Wife, child, sister-in-law and servant wave,
though they might also be dismissing him, pushing him away,
wiping him out of their lives with imaginary dusters,
or holding palms out for their share of his alms.
Now that his business-suited back is turned, they can relax:
mother pours another coffee, crocheted with cream,
and flicks through glossy magazines, winnowing crumbs of toast;
the open window ideal for sunbathing or keeping track of
     neighbours;
the afternoon free for an unmolested nap, when sister gardens
and the infant's pudgy mouth is hushed with jelly beans.

As he bustles back through the front door at night, muttering,
he will find an immaculate cloth set, a hot meal ready.
After hanging his bowler crown up, dabbing his genteel
     moustache,
he will sit, enthroned, at the head of the rectangular table,
permitting the poodle, a foppish courtier, to lick his feet,
throwing it rinds of meat and bread.
And the ladies-in-waiting will pamper him,
bridling their impatience or stifling scorn,
careful not to hassle him like clients
or provoke, like inefficient secretaries, a fit of spleen.

AT THE TOP

In overheated rooms, hung with rustic prints,
they sling jackets off and their sweatlines show.
A dozen identical concrete floors below,
their reserved parking spaces are mapped out.
These are the indispensable men of the world
who know the cost-effectiveness of everything,
who set sales targets and launch new lines,
who sign redundancy notices and dividend cheques
with hands fleshy and tender as cooked chicken legs.
At rush-hour, kaleidoscopes of company cars
clash in the tailbacks of suburban carriageways.
Some stay late, poring over bad debts,
loosening the noose of tie around a forceful neck,
contemplating a change of advertising agency
or adding final touches to the rationalisation plan.
Wars, shortages, strikes can all be put to use.
Even 'futures' can be traded in.
The past is something to be grappled with
when pre-tax profits need to be compared.
Fortune shines on them like bonus issues of shares.

PREMONITIONS

I

Sometimes I stand
in a draught of death:
it wafts through my body

as a premonition
and I shudder like a fridge,
catching its cold.

II

The birth wards swell,
slippery with life,
and every vacancy is filled

so that our absence
will not be noticed
in the changing crowd.

III

This breeze will blow
its loneliness through trees
long after we are shrouded.

Your mourning eyes,
black-rimmed as memorial cards,
will find a deeper sleep.

IV

Each death proves
death still lives,
when lives regular

as breathing stop;
stocking flags triumphant
on the leg-bones' staff.

HOSPITAL

colonnades of patients
daubed with bruises

others coated
with broader strokes

of cancer lemon
hypertension red

like forest trees
branded with paint

for thinning
cutting down

STILLBORN

what we are lamenting
is what has not been
and what will not have seen
this mild May morning

what we are lamenting
is unsuckled air
and what was brought to bear
this mild May morning

what we are lamenting
is the blood and puppy fat, our child,
that has not laughed or cried
this mild May morning

what we are lamenting
is the life we crave
snatched from the cradle to the grave
this mild May morning

DISARMAMENT

your first grey hairs
are plucked out readily enough
and harmony restored

that metal sheen proliferates
and you risk baldness
as you eliminate invaders

NOTE: *A Sile na Gig is a carved female nude, drawing
attention to her genitals, found on medieval buildings
in Britain, France and especially Ireland.*

REPUBLICAN SYMPATHIES

*What I have always liked about the Irish Republic is
that it is, of all the societies that I know, the least
'sexy'*—DONALD DAVIE

It is always raining on this bleak country.
Windows in their rustproof frames are never silent.
Our cottages are damp-proofed to no avail.
Bruise marks of mould deface wallpaper skin.
Smells of decay assail us in our musty sitting-rooms.

How could sexiness survive this purifying climate?
Where would cut-away shoes, see-through blouses,
figure-hugging mini-skirts fit into this arthritic scheme?
Chunky-knits and padded anoraks are the order of the day;
hot-water bottles, flannel bedwear make nights sensuous.

Somewhere, annually, Miss Ireland is announced
and shivers in ciré swimwear just long enough
for ogling lenses to record her nerve.
Occasionally, too, fishnets and high heels are glimpsed,
springing across a bus-stop flood....

Forecasts are seldom good here, bringing forebodings
of worse weather, deteriorating trade, added unemployment.
Days are so dark the end of the world never appears far off.
Hay floats, unharvested, in flooded fields.
The beauty of this land lies mostly in reflection.

Our birth rate stays high (boredom, Vatican encyclicals?):
erotic signals are given off, it seems—muffled
behind layers of ribbed woollen tights, thermal underwear.
What need have we of sex shops, contraceptives?
Yielding Sile na Gigs are cut down to size by an East wind;

summer is a few golden straws to grasp on between showers.

SHOTS

In a rare moment of sunshine, photographer Aidan Heffernan
captured this unusual shot of the Templemore pitch-and-putt
clubhouse—THE TIPPERARY STAR

An unusual shot of the clubhouse
at Templemore pitch-and-putt club
means you see it in a rare sprinkling of sun
through the jagged arch of an old outbuilding.
It is the basic modern bungalow otherwise
with Spanish roll-tile roof, painted fascia,
front door, side door, burglar alarm
(or is that an outside light?)—you might expect
a coal bunker, except no chimney looms.

The concrete blocks strewn along the grass
must be left over from its construction
or are intended, alternatively, to mark
the foundations of some new project
in aid of which a raffle will be organised.
Timber fencing leads along the driveway
to the town where shop business is slack.
The background is shaded in with trees
and, further off, well out of range,

the Devil's Bit hill unfurls its gummy grin,
its Marian Year crucifix a distant fang.
A more usual view of the clubhouse
would, doubtless, require a darker camera setting.
Pustules of wetness would be unleashed
with each measured swipe of a golf stick.
Recruits from the local Garda Training Centre
would be stooping in out of the weather,
their short hair plastered dark and flat.

IN THE PICTURE

It is a perfect painting.
Its lines all run straight.
Its square shape forms an exact square.
Its colours stand strong and pure.
Its surface is without a flaw.
It hangs above ecstasy and sorrow.
It needs no immune system or reassurance.
It is too content to seek pleasure.

The eye is led then
to the white speck of paint
misplaced in an area
of homogenised red.

It is with the speck
that I identify.

A LIFE STUDY

Here is a woman on a bus
half-way through a book
entitled simply *Life*.

I squint, but cannot decipher
who the author is
or what it is about.

She seems to be enjoying it
or is too absorbed at least
to look out at shoppers

wrapped up in their thoughts.
How is *Life* classified?
Fiction, allegory, myth?

Is she dying to know
the kind of ending it will have?
The book slams unexpectedly;

she gets off at the next stop.

AT KILLYKEEN

Such glowing of grass
and plopping of fish
and lapping of water
and sauntering of cattle
and loosening of leaves
mottled as petrified rock....
The late year rallies
for another few days
and musters forces
of bees and midges
and weightless butterflies
for the last raids
before winter infiltrates.
Watch that seabird
skim like a dandelion puff
above the lake,
the shiny forehead of which
is barely creased.
Peace, I suppose,
is the word for this,
for so much buzzing and beating
and screeching and splashing;
or for what this interlude
means to us:
grapes on the wooden balcony;
a Schubert string quintet
as we fix on a line
of nettle-dense pines;
or just this overview
of the chromium lake,
slaking a feverish thirst
we have carried with us
through the citified year.
A hare among ferns at dawn.
Now a heron hunched against sunset.
I toss a stone into the water
to see how deep it goes.

CALF

If it is being fattened for food,
if there are people with recipes for veal
who would steal the spring from its step

or rip the stitching of its meat apart
or promote profit-growth through hormones,
the calf won't pause to contemplate such things.

If it understood words, it would not prate
about hoose, brucellosis, bovine t.b.
or the level of E.E.C. farm grants.

What it knows of the world at the moment
prompts it to run for joy, to prance,
to flap a tagged ear, swish a stippled tail.

I am reminded of it as I watch a child
with eager eyes, dainty dress, miniature rucksack,
pony-tail, hand sheltered in her mother's palm,

skipping down the street in front of me.
And I realise my own feet, dragging me to work,
have not been inspired to jump for joy in years.

INEDIBLE ANECDOTES

I

and he created Adam and then Eve
and he begat their appetites
so that they snapped forbidden fruit
seduced by new tastes more than by knowledge

and then they had to sweat
to earn the bread work led to hunger for

and he grudged them what they swallowed
shoving it down the wrong way
inflaming and perforating the intestines
ulcerating the stomach, distending salivary glands
obstructing the oesophagus, rotting teeth
weight loss or gain symptomatic of disease

II

and he gave us a taste for life
and just enough of love and skill
and friendship and commitment to a place
to make us yearn for more

and he permitted us a glimpse
of the world glittering in the sun
like a fortune-telling crystal ball:
yellow flowers lovely as blood plasma
velvet fields under chandeliers of rain
birds like clothes pins flocking on a line

and as soon as we began to take this life for granted
he mashed us like frogs on a workday road

BIRTHMARKS

we took our places without fuss in the native town
the men on bar stools scarcely looking up
the couples eating ice-cream cones and sweets
peering from cars on the rain-drenched square

what strange unresolved sensations ours were
to look through meatball eyes, to sleep
to feel a chest catch with each breath
and try to draw conclusions from it all

we strained, in turn, for those who had absorbed our genes
our stooped backs, our guilts, our hereditary disease
we passed life among lives that were like railway sidings
where grass grows through narrow lengths of aimless track

our strength was short-lived, broken by heart attacks
    and strokes:
the drift-net of tides we dragged for fish
the offices where we issued reminders
the chip shops where we fed jukeboxes and queued

will be our only lasting monuments
the first posthumous downpour will wash our blood away
our longings will be smothered with ivy
moss will obliterate our names

SPERM

an oil slick polluting her canal
scum of humanity seed of pain

dense multiple warheads
arms racing to strike target terrain

the triumphant achieve spina bifida
or ambition malnutrition or fame

and hundreds of millions of tiny sprigs
are marketed in vain

a lost civilisation
a bedclothes stain

SPOILED CHILD

my child recedes inside me
and need never puzzle where it came from
or lose a football in the dusty laurel bushes
or sneak change from my jacket to buy sweets

my child will not engage in active military service
or make excuses about its school report
or look up from a picture book, dribbling a pink smile
or qualify for free glasses or school lunch

my child will not become a prodigy of musicianship or crime
and will evince no appetite for hamburgers or drugs
and will suffer neither orgasm nor kidney stones
reduced neither to a statistic nor a sacrifice

my child will not play space games with its cousins
or sit adrift on a grandparent's lap
or slit its wrists or erect a loving headstone on my grave
or store a secret name for frogs or treetops

my child will not be a comfort to my old age
my child will not be cheated or promoted or denied
my child will trail me, like a guardian angel, all my life
its blemishes, its beauty, its shortcomings and its promise

forever unsullied and unfulfilled

BRIEF LIVES

I

after the house has been pilfered
the private things fingered
and a phone call poses a new threat

after your child's accident affects your sales drive
the smear test turns out positive
and your worst fears are confirmed again

how should you spend the next day, the rest of your life
what keeps you going—cowardice, forgetfulness or hope
what is it you are impelled towards

II

so many hurt feelings and frustrated desires
toast- and coffee-scented pleasures also
at fires grinding into muesli ash

so many seconds harnessed to just being
years and decades consolidating to experience
it takes an eternity to recover from them all

III

the calm between storms
is the silence in which
the dead are not named
until relatives are informed

IV

in the end death worries only bones

CONTRACTS

after Paul Celan

I   IRISCH

Grant me ingress
to your night
to count sheep,
permission to transverse
your dream slopes,
the turbary rights
of your heart's peat,
in perpetuity.

II   DU WARST

You were my only loophole
in the repressive act of death:

my last exemption clause.

THE UNITIES

I   SIAMESE

I stand in the field of your vision
I perceive with the light of your experience
I drink from the stream of your consciousness

our skins are grafted into one
when you eat I am nourished
when I kiss you I am kissed

friends complain they cannot see us separately
and have warned about
dire complications likely to arise

when the first one of us dies

II   ONE PLUS ONE

my fears for you are spontaneous as disasters
insistent as an ambulance bearing the bad news
frenzied as blue police lights palpitating
obsessed as metal cutters biting through sealed doors
irrepressible as the black tear of a funeral

and my love is spontaneous as simple arithmetic
insistent as figures multiplying on a screen
frenzied as circuits of veins across software
obsessed as sperm are with calculations
irrepressible as the recurring decimal of sex

'O MY AMERICA!'

The few U.S.-published kids' books
in the Thurles library
felt and smelt as differently
from the usual Puffins and Antelopes
as Tipperary does from Illinois.
We were growing apart
before growing together,
not knowing yet
what in the world we would be
when we grew up:
me straggling from school
with a Milroy macaroon bar,
your small lips smothered
by Hershey's Kisses.
It is fall—not autumn—
in this children's book.
Trees bulge in a wind
that dusts the grass off,
polishing its surface.
A little dog, ears flying,
leaps up to unwinding leaves
as if sniffing the offal
of a dying year.
The boys are given crew cuts
in 'full-color illustrations';
they wear plaid lumber jackets
and scream names into the storm
that sound like Chuck and Chester.
No one answers to your name
among the Cathy Annes and Debbies,
until a freckled girl is seen
waving from a slatted house,
her hair in braids,
her smooth face notched with dimples:
she could be the one
whose photograph I cherish
in my wallet now.

TIME-SHARING

In our time together
we are travelling in the heated car,
a violin concerto playing on the radio,
hills streaming with winter cold,
year-end fields worn down to seams,
a blazing quiff of distant dogwood,
burned meringue of snow on mountain tops.

We blurt past farms and cottages:
those whose era we share
are staring from net curtains
at a morning chill for milking
or for setting off to factories in the town,
their segments of road deserted.
It is like a childhood journey

of sleep and open-eyed surprise,
of hermetically sealed life
in the eternal present
before the final destination is reached.
We hold hands on the gear stick
and, at this moment,
fear for nothing except the future.

DEVOTIONS

I

both relished the yield
of the tree of carnal knowledge
and, like God, learned to procreate

her apple breasts enticed
stiff nipple nails sank
as they lost paradise

II

at mass you spread your tongue out
for communion
your lips lustrous with wine

I adore your wafer-pale host
that will diffuse its ether slowly
as its seal breaks

III

because beauty will not last
and time dismantles every mystery
I savour your divineness

and through your shallow skin
the stub of an angel's wing protrudes
damaged in your fall

IV

in the red light of our sanctuary
a real presence is felt

the deep wound that I touch
uplifts me beyond doubt

and we kiss with a gift of tongues
and forget how Jesus was betrayed

DAY AND NIGHT

I

wrapped in a sheer white negligée
    you are a fog-bound landscape
familiar but seen in a new light
    transformed by seamless mist
tantalising, trimmed with tufts of cloud
    I know that after the fog lifts
all will be sultry and warm
    I can detect a sun-like breast
already radiating through the nylon dawn

II

in hot darkness, the transistor on
    a five-note raga plays
five senses that ascend the scale of longing:
    until the gasps of music peter out
and a taut night is plucked limp
    we are out of meaning's reach
your vellum blotted with invisible ink
    my head at rest
between your breasts' parentheses

CALENDAR GIRLS

An artist might respond to these appeals of flesh,
screened through lace and fishnet,
and give them permanent refuge
in small brushstrokes of paint.
The models were careless of their absolute power,
heedless of what a shake-out of hair
or a casual baring of limbs could induce.

And their lewd men were heedless
of the frailty of what they coveted,
how perishable it was, how much its contents
would sag and settle during transit
as, month by sun-drenched month,
girls went into decline,
the passage of their time recorded,

ticking away, like high heels, at their feet.

INFIDELITY

What O'Driscoll needs is what Leopold Bloom frankly adores: the
'ample, bedwarmed flesh' of Molly Bloom. For he lacks credence
in the body, its sweetness and plenty—THE IRISH TIMES

they are letting us down, the bedwarmed women
being let down themselves into beds of clay
that swallowed Molly Bloom and Milly Bloom
those who fed our grandfathers' fantasies and our own
those who combed the library shelves for historical romances

those whose shining eyes solicited the darker sides of streets
those who were the fertile ground where ancestral seeds fell
those who held their flesh at arm's length
and those with gyrating bodies bandaged in tight jeans
only bony fingers left to caress your thinning scalp

gone those posing for sepia photographs and cheap videos
all the old loves that haunted your marriage becoming ghosts
all let down by their flesh, bra cups emptied, basques unbound
all those around whose necks possessive hands coiled
those doing nature's work or god's, lay sisters or unmarried
    mums

they are topless now, stripped of flesh that had all-over tan
their bodies creased with household wear and tear
serene behind the mortician's heavy make-up:
and after their brief orbit of the globe
silent as the ovum's mysterious rotations

they are brought gently down to earth

THURLES

after Zbigniew Herbert

A childhood too boring for words
is lost without a fragment in that town.
And, so, I have held my tongue about its gutturals;
its sky slated consistently with cloud;
its mossy roofs restraining excesses of rain.

One house watches out for me, though.
I know where its cabbage colander is kept
and the special knack required to use its tin-opener
and the exact key in which the kitchen door,
scuffed by a ring-board, creaks:

things I cannot depict in dictionary terms,
through heartless words that fail to resonate.
Others are suppressed in embarrassment or pain
(all families have passed their own equivalents
to the Official Secrets Act).

Yet everything there translates into feeling:
the plates the dead have eaten from before us,
the layers of wallpaper that still pattern memory,
the hairline crack in marble that was my fault,
the rose-arched garden explored down to its last stone.

Back in the city, I resort to standard words again.
Unable to identify possessions by their first names,
I call them only by their surnames
—by their brand names—
and will never discover their real names.

THE OPEN MARKET

The estate agents' glossy lists
provocatively insist
on their monopolies of 'luxury' and 'charm'
(meaning made-up whited sepulchres
teeming with woodworm and dry rot…).

'Choosy clients', 'discerning buyers'
are titillated by the allurements:
'mature', 'desirable', 'appealing',
'well-built', 'attractive features',
'much sought-after location'.

House-hunting, I occupy myself
reading between the cracks
these leaflets paper over:
'great potential', 'requires upgrading',
'old-world atmosphere'.

There must be a tree some place
that can accommodate my 'dream home'
('beams exposed', 'breathtaking views',
'not overlooked'), where worms and grubs
are 'converted' into music by the birds.

HOME AFFAIRS

I

Death is moving into newly-constructed suburbs,
through semi-detached houses, ugly identical twins.
Hired cars will call for widows who had come as brides....

Where readymix cement ejects from giant hair-driers,
the foundations of our married lives are laid.
We will slice the keyhole loaf of bread together here.

This evening, a rainbow unfolded its colour chart
and I imagined these dwellings once painted, tamed:
the knock of radiators in a dry-lined sitting room;

whispers and bickerings filtered through air vents;
the small-hour lulls only the troubled sleepers know
or babysitters waiting for the owners to reach home.

II

Dashed housefronts gleam like popcorn, a mirage
seen from what will be the main road through estates,
bearing working couples, coal deliveries or crowded bus,
pavements reserved for tricycles, shopping trollies, prams.

We are strolling on its asphalt arc, a desert airstrip
covering ancient cow-tracks, smoothing paths,
a digger's tyre marks—arrowheads—along its verge.
All we will reap from now on in this raw settlement

are plastic piping, gypsum board and brick.
Our new fridges and washing machines will rust
in mountains of our indestructible sediment,
our baths end up as drinking troughs.

In the distempered house, we try to appear civilised,
use silvery bins, hang prints, keep carpets swept,
at evening listen to symphonies, or read,
hearing container trucks along the dual carriageway.

With a poker for sword, a fireguard for shield,
you provoke the blazing fangs to fume and spit.
Will they know peace who sit quietly in their own rooms?
I trace the braille goosebumps of your body

and begin to lip-read as the night intensifies.

III

It is an ordinary morning without pain.
Sun's spotlight stares from a dishevelled sky,
ruffled with clouds like a safety curtain.
Summer is in heat again: gooseberry scrotums swell,
hard blackberry knuckles will soon ooze with blood.

The window swings out on to a butterfly-light breeze,
a heady aura of sweet peas, rose fumes, poppy seasoning.
Cut lawns exude fresh hay; grasshopper blades whirr;
resinous smells of wood pervade the tool shed.
No bad news breaks today, no sudden tragedy, no urgent
    telegrams,

no hospital visiting, no pacing outside intensive care units.
The sun blossoms in its foliage of cloud
and we fortify ourselves with its light, our house's silence,
against the trouble, bustle, pain
which other mornings will, irrevocably, bring.

AFTERTHOUGHTS

what we hanker after is hope
the way a patient is propped up in bed
to take solid food after drip-fed weeks

what we seek is reassurance
after our parents' secure grip has slackened
like an undertaker's band
and our marriage vows ring hollow as delf
on the sloped, stainless-steel draining board

hope and reassurance
—while death runs in families
like blood in urine—

that like the grit on winter tyres
like the missing shirt button
like the loose dewdrops of a thaw
that nothing disappears forever
that childhood's prospect can be sustained

that our ten thousand brain components razed each day
that our dreams drilled by pneumatic snores
that our stamped-on feet and elbowed torsos

mean something more than themselves
that the bones of death will not outcreak our lives:
and we pry for consolation in books and stars and test tubes
the way I searched my dead father's pockets
to assemble clues, to measure his life's change

BREVIARY

STORM

a vein of lightning slits the sky
discharges a haemorrhage of rain

IDOLATRY

the strawberry is a sacred heart
a tooth here is a foot in heaven

HOSPITAL

between pre-natal and mortuary
the research unit

MANNA

a yolk of moon
its shell speckled with stars

ARS POETICA

butchers put price tags on meat
or neatly trim the fat around its edge

ARS EDITORIA

each body of work is tested by the surgeon
for the regularity of its beat:
he scans it thoroughly for jarring rhythms, stress
rejects superfluous appendices and checks the x-ray's proofs

his failures are remaindered, their circulation stopped

NIGHT WATCH

to get to sleep
he started to count sheep
but they too were
being led to the slaughter

EVERGREEN

God perches at the apex
of his star-decorated tree

a Christmas fairy
that can withhold or grant our wish

waving wand or stick
conducting the music of the spheres

HERITAGE

what looks like chalk dust
floats down from the blackboard sky

knee-deep in its white detritus
children climb out from the rubble

where killed friends and teachers lie
and try to build a snowman

THE FATHER

after William Carlos Williams

so much depends
upon the familiar sound
of his red car

coming at night
around the final bend
toward home

scattering white chickens
and shattering glazed puddles
of rain

Part Two

Kist poems
for Michael Hamburger

KIST

(i.m. 14th February 1975)

On that lovers' morning, our hearts chimed.
Later, the slow death knell of hers
and a coffin door slamming
in her last chill breath.

Preparing me for your death, then,
I noticed silver strands,
coffin-handle bright,
beneath your oak-brown hair.

And, pacing behind hearse,
my own face in its glass
took on the wrinkled grain
of coffin wood.

ELEGIES

I

sapling
that was rooted
at his birth

is ready to yield
a coffin now:
its rings

like ripples spread
to count
his submerged years

II

we are digging
on this spring day
burying an exhausted gardener

his stiffly-folded
cigarette-stained fingers
brown as clay

the weeping cherry
he planted
beginning to bud

III

a snowdrop host
our only solid food
melts in the mouth

we are drunk
on altar wine
a rare blood group

seeking strength to face
the gathering crowds
of dead

IV

he is stored
in the gold bullion
of an oak coffin

overhead the earth's scars heal
flowers are dyeing fields
a road worker is in full song

and only we can tell
that sunlight casts
one shadow less

SIBLINGS

I am writing at exactly the moment
you had sent me the message of his death
precisely this time last year.

Returning home from school to an empty house,
you have begun to live your own lives with the vulnerability
of those who know how thin the barrier of flesh is,

that looking forward becomes looking back
until there is nothing either way but death.
It is quiet in the office as I write,

hiding this paper under a file,
heat rising from radiators, first cigarettes being lit,
someone whistling, someone listing soccer scores.

We have spent a year without him now,
his thoughts scattered, his burden of organs eased.
This is just another working day here

of queries, letters, tea-breaks, forms.
Any minute now some telephone will ring
but I do not dread its news, as then.

I concentrate upon this moment, cup it in my hands,
to understand what the shedding of his skin might signify
and what you have lost in these past years

in which home has become orphanage
and we have soiled the carpet in the hall
with the clay of their two burials,

our world refracted by a lens of tears.

TRACES

I

time sieves us into dust
our residue is gall-stone, bone
flesh offers no protection
elbow and back wear through its fabric

II

beneath the surface of our lives
skin deep is buried death
(like underwear we carry skeletons
folded neatly in our trunks)

III

its name is signed
between lines of forehead
in calligraphy of ribs
shakily on wet cardiogram, last will

IV

even from padded cells of brain
life eventually escapes
bones like scaffolding mark sites
where flesh walls stood

CONTENTS

I   BLOOD

gravy flowing through raw meat
red jam that sets in clots
hot running water the heart pumps

II   HEART

a rigged-up plug
its cable arteries
connect us to life

but like a fuse it blows
turning the mind's light out
freezing the body's rooms

III   SKIN

heat-freckled, blushing with emotion
tucked into pleats and curves

erupting into milk-pink tapioca of cold
perfumed, painted, stained with birth or beatings

layered with ills, stitched with hairs
glimpsed through incubator or blouse

it is the litmus paper
of perishable, sensitive, volatile lives

the tent we pitch inside
huddling around heart's fire

IV   BRAIN

brassica swelling
from the leafy cerebellum

the sacral nerves
rooted like cruciferae

V

*(on the day a man received
the heart of a schoolgirl donor)*

the house is flooded
with unexpected sunshine
I wade through light

it is a day
for short sleeves, sandals
for a change of heart

feeling the throb
of a sixteen-year-old
schoolgirl's joy

inside me

73

BEING

I   CONCEPTION

juice of being is squeezed from a ripe body
aspiring with orgasmic joy to life
its bean sprouts hanging by a thread
to dreams of soccer leagues, investment bonds, mince pies

past chiffon folds of mucus
a spoon of sperm cracks open a moon egg
buries a head in its sand
finds its atmosphere habitable

a fossil brands the womb now
the prehistoric zip of spine, the lizard tail
the hard imprint of bone
frozen in molten fluids

in the opening scene
a couple walked the strand
a child's first cry will be
the sadness they feel after coition

II   ENTROPY

from the womb everything appeared beautiful
he swam, a goldfish, in the plastic water bag
peering with big eyes
behind the flimsy curtain,

a swollen bubble he longed to pierce:
but now the dented head
becomes a heavy globe
balanced on tilting axis of spine

his nerves, high-tension wires,
bear messages of fear
it is not enough to be a miracle
of raspberry taste-buds and bladder greens

an ambulance siren
divides the city traffic
he has drowned his organs in poison
and rushes, sperm-swift, towards premeditated death

III   HEART

amplified in the cardiac unit
the businessman's heart is deafening
as the first bang of creation
its valves flap open on a fibreglass moth's wing

artery walls are daubed in cholesterol and smoke
and heart's pothole is choked in clots
curdled blood begins to slake
its insatiable mouth

and it misses the note of life
broadcasting alarm hoarsely
through the loudhailer of stethoscope
its morse tapping an emergency code:

in the operating theatre
light enters tunnels, ventricles, again
heart smacks its rosy lips
revived by a trickling saliva of blood

IV BRAIN

a fig-leaf of skin
hides the shameful serpent of intestines
our parcel of flesh is tied
with nerve ends and veins

over which is coiled
the brain's grey rope
a meaty sandwich spread
a cushioned seat of wisdom

preserved under a cracked ceiling
with the pineal body ('site of the soul')
cloud puffy
dreamy between hemispheres

and sometimes cords are purposely snapped
brain's knotted pâté is sliced
or electric shocks
singe troubling memories

V SKELETON

when tight skirt of skin,
a body stocking, is threadbare
and wickerwork of muscle
unwinds from biceps and thigh

like elastic dressing, mummy-cloth
our classical interior is revealed
carved bust of skull
marble pillars of bone

and pictures painted in blood fade
from the cranium's cave
knowledge, love and dread are emptied
the meat machine halts production

and salted tide of life ebbs
in which foetus gills thrived
leaving a landscape of calcium rocks
our solid foundation stones

VI   DEATH

what will be our certified cause of death
will we expire with the lost memory of arteriosclerosis
dissolving in alcohol, crumbling with pain
basted in our own body fat, shivering with old age

our distilled water polluted by cancer, angina, rash
until we resign work and life and suffering
all family fights over, love consummated, arguments resolved
the patiently accumulated facts forgotten:

the bouquet of heart we offered partners withers
its petalled rose shrivels, its valves harden into thorns
fresh cream of breasts sours, dream topping of skin acidifies
cherry nipples turn to pips

the clock is a wheel of fortune
each second leads to separate destinies
its thin compass-needle hands
direct us, pilot us from time

VII   THROUGH THE MICROSCOPE

the long flowing tresses of a fallopian tube
the crazy paving of cells
the stained-glass window of hormone crystals
the abstract canvas of a city dweller's lung

the rainfall of erected hair
the stranded dolphin of a nerve
the flaming snout of the pulmonary vein
the gaping volcanoes of the colon

the butter yellow of cholesterol
the stratified rock of cones and rods
the magnified saliva of a gourmet
the decayed tooth of racial superiority

the drained kidney of egotism
the white vocal chords of politics like gleaming fangs
the roots of wit and sarcasm inexplicable
the binding agent of life still unidentified

SOMEONE

someone is dressing up for death today, a change of skirt or tie
eating a final feast of buttered sliced pan, tea
scarcely having noticed the erection that was his last
shaving his face to marble for the icy laying out
spraying with deodorant her coarse armpit grass
someone today is leaving home on business
saluting, terminally, the neighbours who will join in
     the cortège
someone is trimming his nails for the last time, a precious
     moment
someone's thighs will not be streaked with elastic in the future
someone is putting out milkbottles for a day that will not
     come
someone's fresh breath is about to be taken clean away
someone is writing a cheque that will be marked 'drawer
     deceased'
someone is circling posthumous dates on a calendar
someone is listening to an irrelevant weather forecast
someone is making rash promises to friends
someone's coffin is being sanded, laminated, shined
who feels this morning quite as well as ever
someone if asked would find nothing remarkable in today's
     date
perfume and goodbyes her final will and testament
someone today is seeing the world for the last time
as innocently as he had seen it first